BOTANIMALS

VOLUME 1

A COLORING BOOK

OF

FLORA AND FAUNA

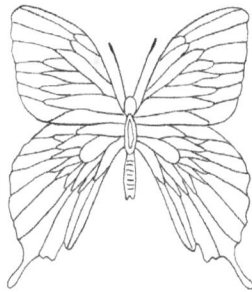

ILLUSTRATED BY

JENNIFER LINDERMAN

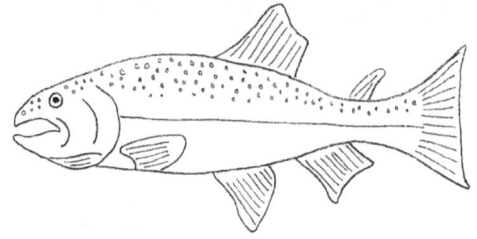

Published in 2016 by
Createspace Publishing
4900 LaCross Road
North Charleston, SC
29406

ISBN: 978-0-692-80226-7

This book belongs to:

_____

Dedication

This book would not be possible without the inspiration
and support of my husband,
Ryan and my two precious children,
Max and Sophie.

I am eternally grateful to my parents and their encouragement
for me to explore the road less traveled.

Special thanks to my Origami students
who help spark my best project ideas and
whose laughter gets me out of bed each morning!

Last but not least, Palesa Nicolini, I am forever
in your debt for your impeccable sense of design and
candid suggestions along the way!

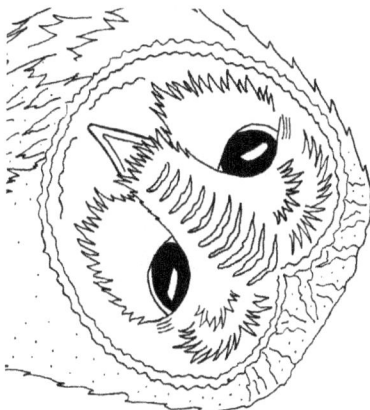

Within the pages of this book
you will find yourself
in the company of an assortment
of plants and animals from
around the world.

Each plant and animal
has been carefully chosen
and artfully rendered
to represent a relationship
to one another.

There are several unique pattern pages
included which can be used for a
variety of things such as
gift wrap, envelope liners or
Origami objects.

Use the botanic drawings
on the following three pages
to see if you can discover
the hidden meanings!

Foxglove

Tiger Lily

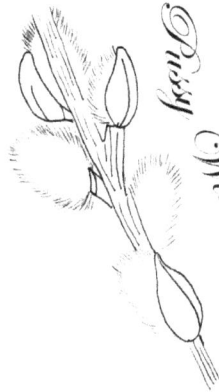

Pussy Willow

*Dogwood
Blossom*

*Bear Grass
Bud*

Horsetail

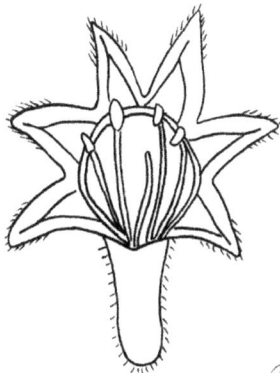

Kangaroo Paw Plant Flower

Goatsbeard

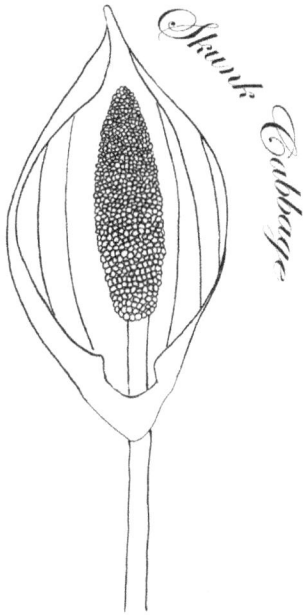

Skunk Cabbage

Kangaroo Paw Plant

Dogwood Seed Pod

Horsemint

Pig's Ear Succulent

Wisteria Seed Pod

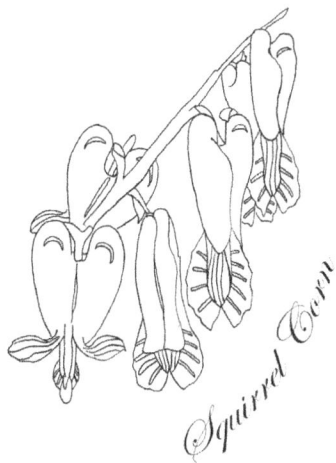

Squirrel Corn

Deer Grass

Owl Clover

Hens and Chicks Succulent

Bird of Paradise

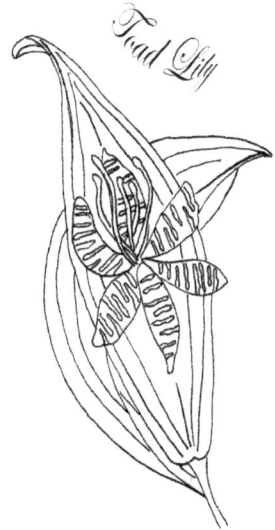

Toad Lily

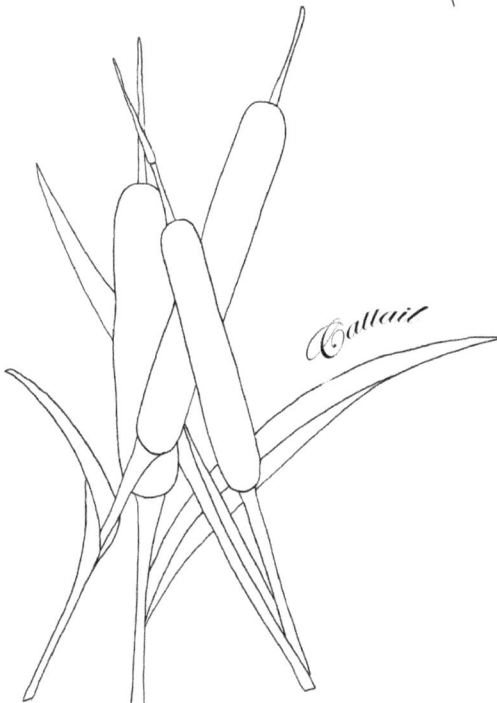

Cattail

Bear Grass

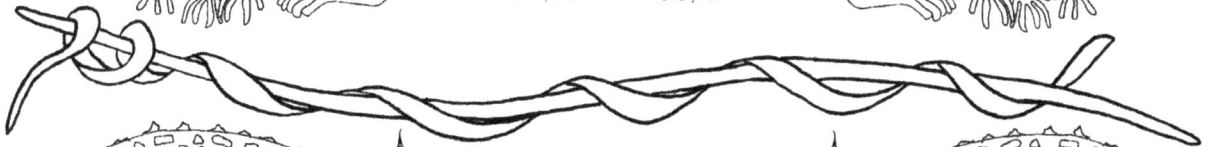

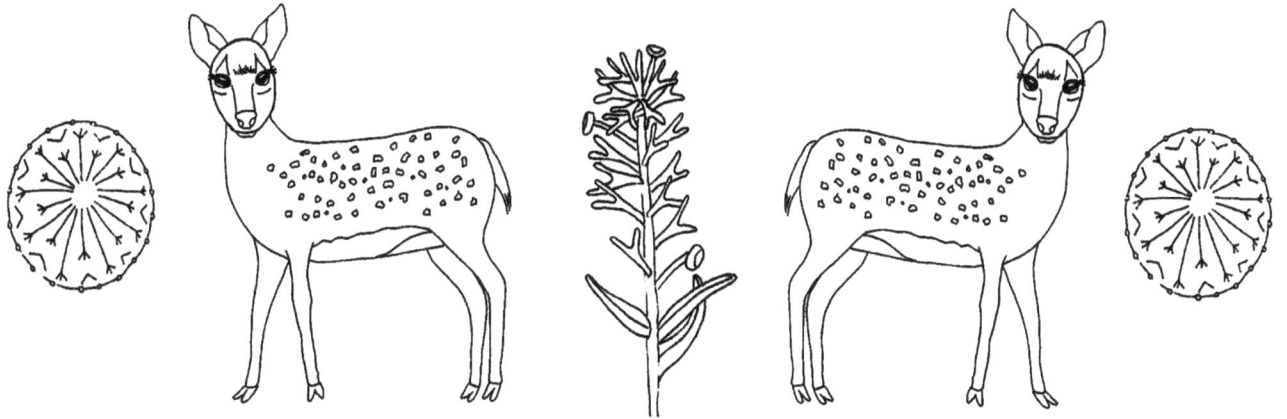

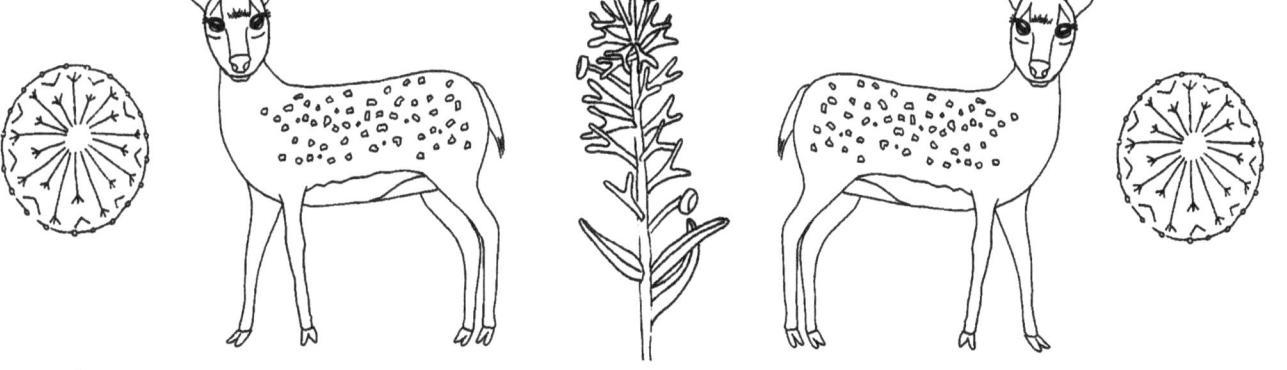

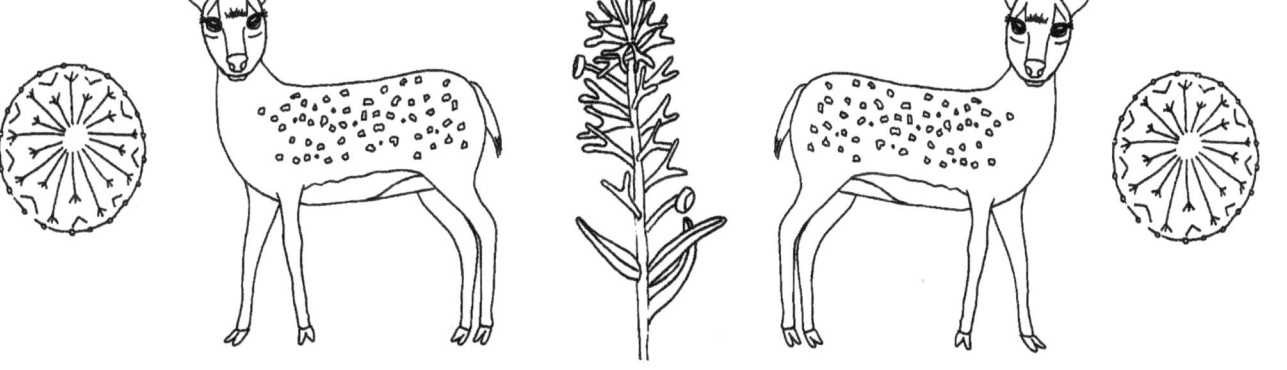

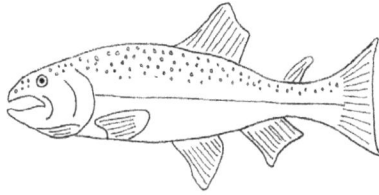

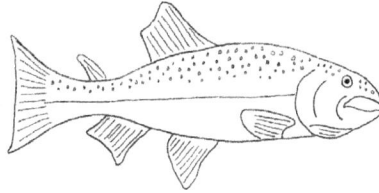

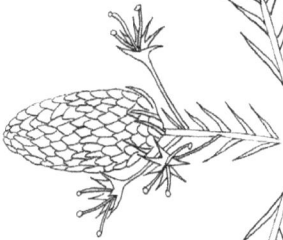

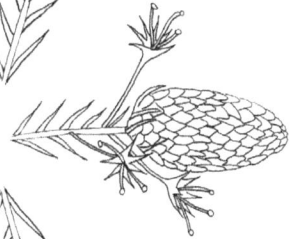

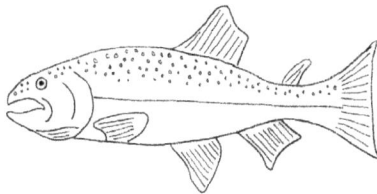

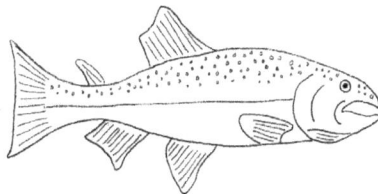

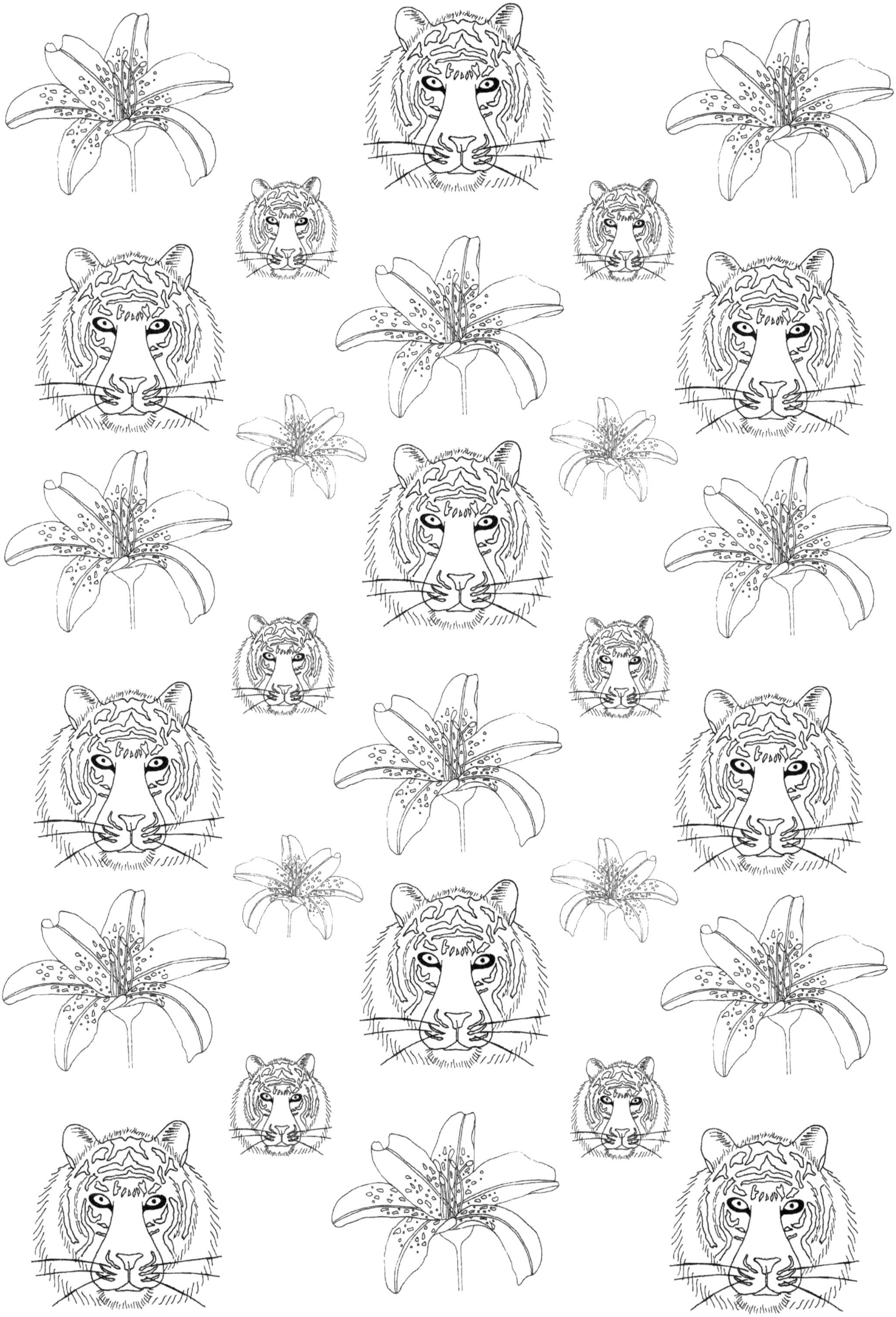

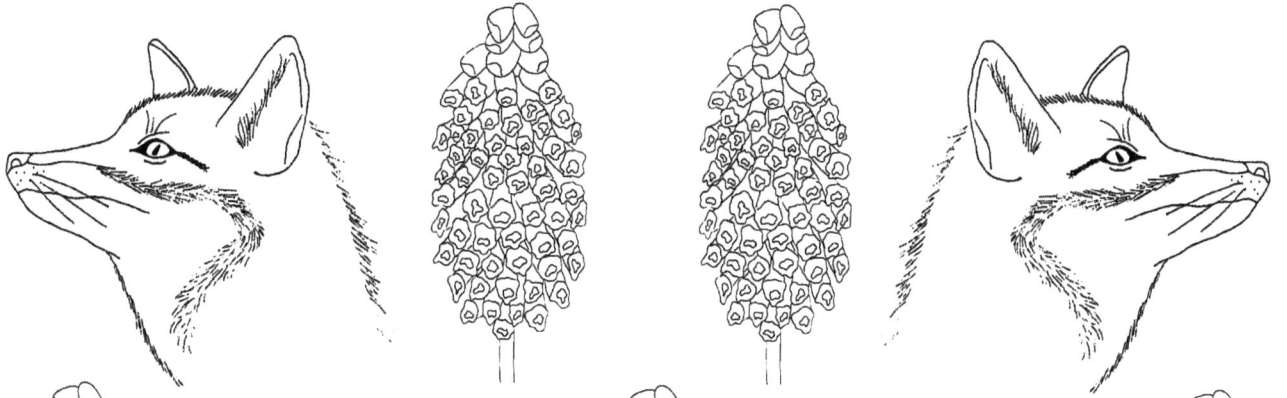

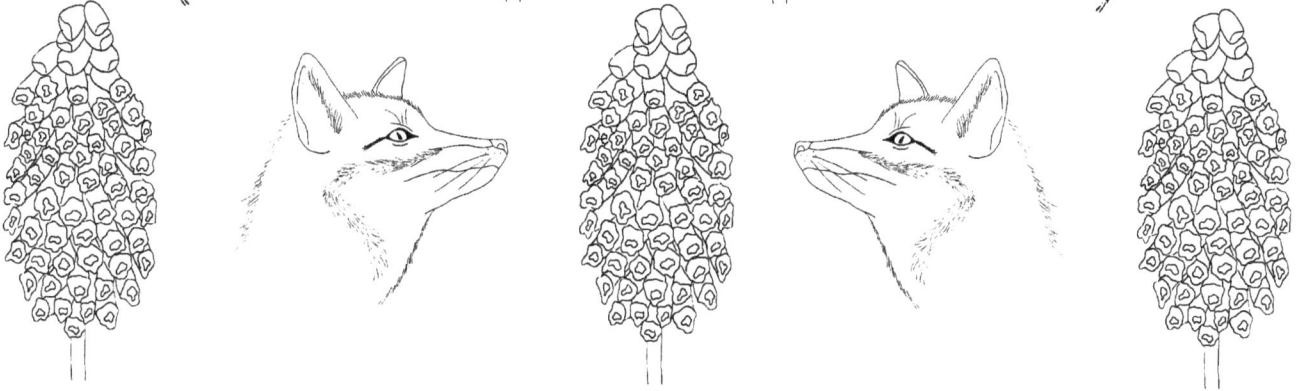

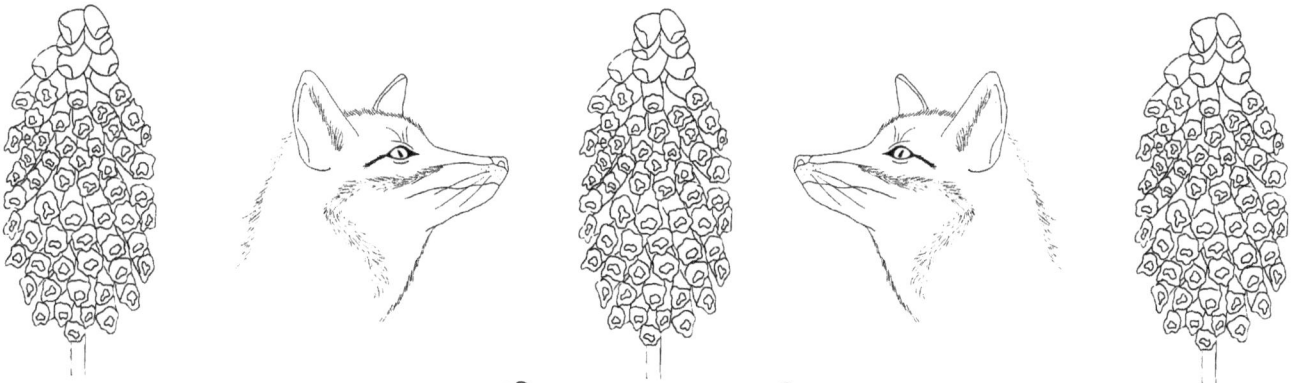

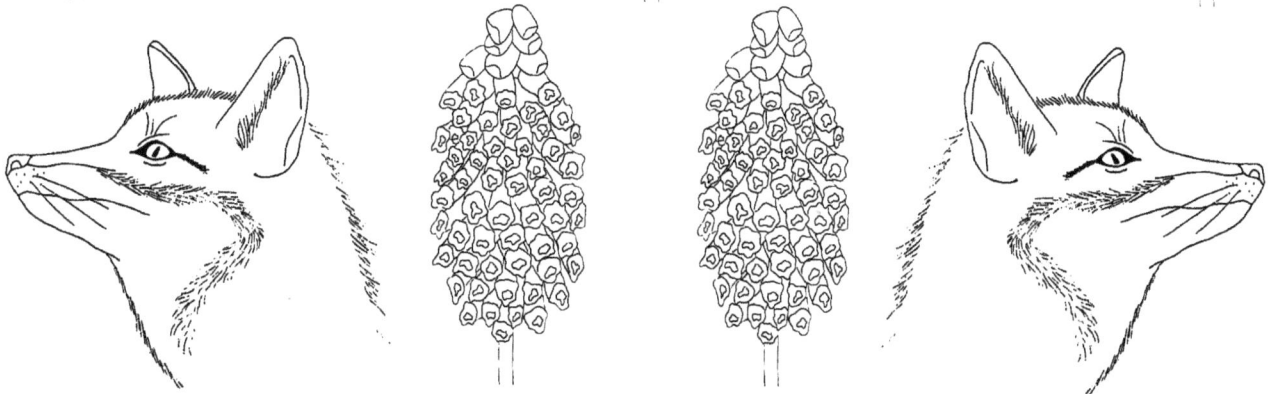

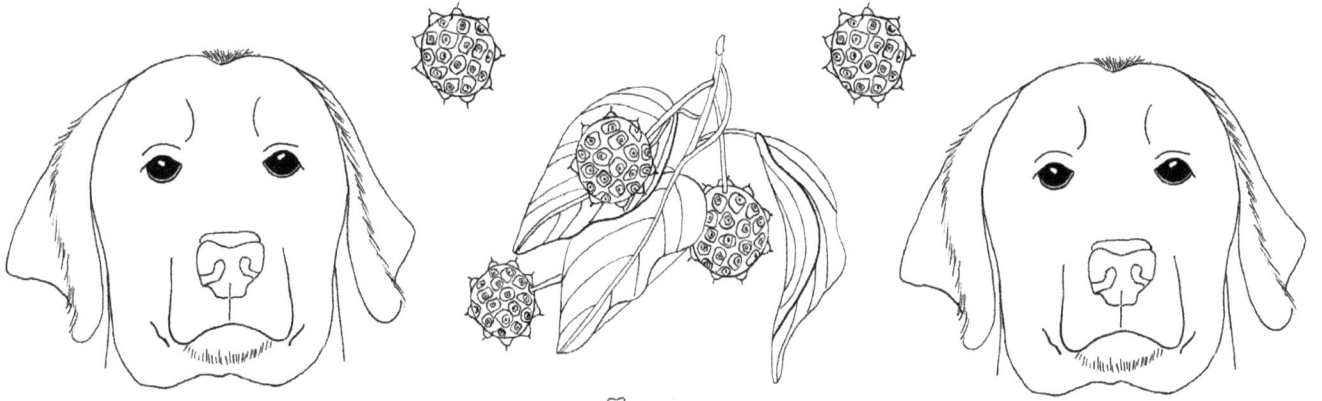

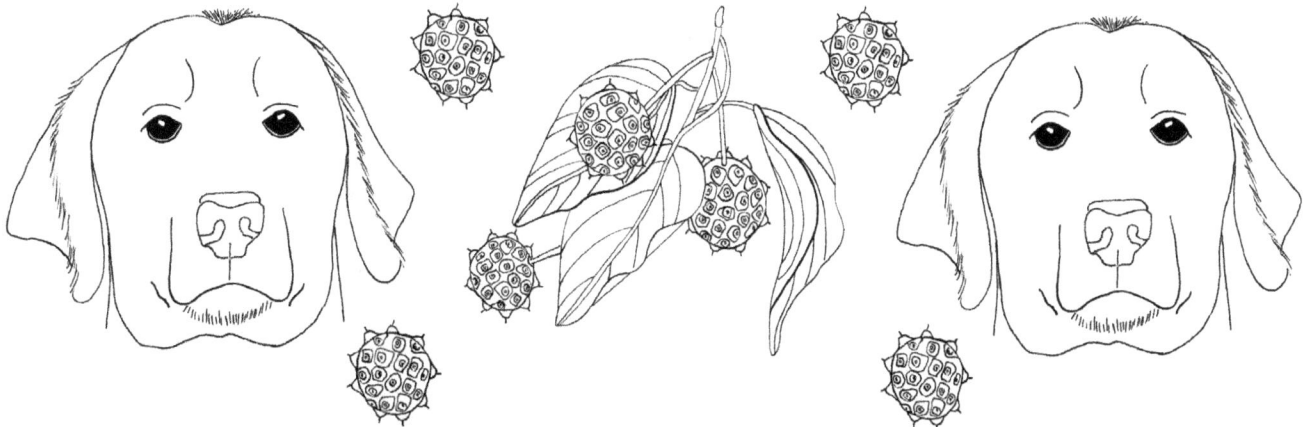

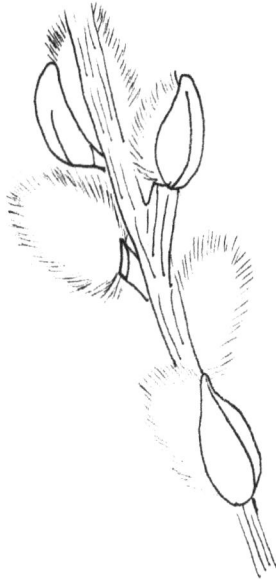

About the Author

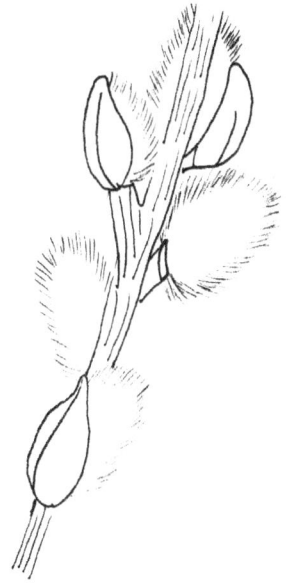

Jennifer Linderman is a self-taught artist and
illustrator living in Oakland, California
with her husband and two children.

Jennifer owns her own business, "Origami
Mami" where she teaches Origami to elementary
school-aged children as an After School program
throughout the East Bay.

She has a particular passion for themes in nature
which are evident in much of her artwork.

You can find more of Jennifer's work on her website:

www.jenniferlindermanart.com

Follow her on Facebook, Instagram and Twitter

www.ingramcontent.com/pod-product-compliance
Lightning Source LLC
Chambersburg PA
CBHW081701270326
41933CB00017B/3232